INTO THE WILDERNESS

Singing Once Again

Alexander Salcido

INTO THE WILDERNESS

Singing Once Again

Alexander Salcido

Copyright © 2025 Alexander Salcido
All rights reserved.
Unless otherwise identified, Scripture quotations are from the New King James Version.

All emphasis within Scripture quotations is the author's own.

Specific pronouns in Scripture that refer to the Father, Son, and Holy Spirit will be capitalized.

The New King James Version (1982). Thomas Nelson. Peterson, E. H. (2005).

The Message: the Bible in contemporary language, NavPress.

The New International Version (NIV) 1984 is an English Bible translation published in 1978 by Biblica (formerly the International Bible Society)

The Holy Bible: King James Version (Electronic Edition of the 1900 Authorized Version, Ge). (2009). Logos Research Systems, Inc.

Holy Bible, New Living Translation, copyright © 1996, 2004, 2015 by Tyndale House Foundation.

ACKNOWLEDGEMENTS

I extend my deepest gratitude to my Lord and Savior, Jesus Christ, who alone deserves all glory, honor, and power. By His grace, I have become the person I am today. In His sovereignty, God chose to pour His heavenly treasures into this earthen vessel. Jesus, a million thanks.

I would also like to express my deepest gratitude to my pastors, Thomas and Dora Alvarez. Their profound influence on my spiritual growth has been immeasurable. Their unwavering devotion to God, family, souls, and prayer has shaped me into the person I am today. The tangible manifestation of their sacrifice and love is immortalized in the annals of heaven, and their impact on my life will forever be cherished.

"Pastor Tommy Alvarez, A man of Prayer, A Man Apart." - Alex Salcido

TABLE OF CONTENTS

Introduction	1
CHAPTER ONE	
Lured into the wilderness	7
CHAPTER TWO	
Comfort in the desert	13
CHAPTER THREE	
Vineyards in the wilderness	19
CHAPTER FOUR	
A door of hope	23
CHAPTER FIVE	
Singing once again	28
CHAPTER SIX	
From Master to Husband	33
CHAPTER SEVEN	
The husband's call	39
CHAPTER EIGHT	
Disciplines that make my life	44
CHAPTER NINE	
Author's biography	55
CHAPTER TEN	
Additional resources	59

INTO THE WILDERNESS

Singing Once Again

"The heart is the instrument of our vocation

So when our heart is breaking, we must labor with a broken tool."

- John Piper

"Therefore, behold, I will allure her, and bring her into the wilderness, and speak comfortably unto her. And I will give her her vineyards from thence, and the valley of Achor for a door of hope: and she shall sing there, as in the days of her youth, and as in the day when she came up out of the land of Egypt. And it shall be at that day, saith the LORD, that thou shalt call me Ishi; and shalt call me no more Baali" (Hosea 2:14-16, KJV).

INTRODUCTION

"Into the Wilderness" recounts an encounter I had in my relationship with God, which provided the solution to a growing dissatisfaction in my life. At times, even when external circumstances seem favorable and tangible achievements are evident, we may still feel unfulfilled, unhappy, and even perplexed. It was here that God led me into the wilderness, where nothing stood between us but our connection. At that moment, God gained my undivided attention, allowing Him to speak comfort to me, illuminate my soul, and lift my spirit.

The wilderness I'm referring to is a growing dissatisfaction that can sometimes follow victories in our lives. I call it the "Desert of Dissatisfaction." While the wilderness is often associated with defeat and dryness during hard times, the wilderness I found myself in occurred during external victories in my life, family, and ministry. I invite you to join me on this journey, culminating in a whole new revelation of God's love and favor.

This book draws inspiration from the Book of Hosea, highlighting the prophet's ministry to the northern kingdom of Israel during a period of apparent prosperity and growth. Despite these outward appearances, moral corruption and spiritual unfaithfulness were widespread among the people. Throughout his half-century of prophetic ministry, Hosea consistently conveyed a threefold message: God detests the sins of His people; judgment is inevitable; yet, **God's steadfast love remains unwavering.** This forms the central context of the book of Hosea.

"Therefore, behold, I will allure her, will bring her into the wilderness, and speak comfort to her" (Hosea 2:14).

> Get alone with Jesus, and He will comfort your hearts and restore your weary souls."
> - Charles Spurgeon

As my ministry has spanned over three and a half decades, I have witnessed both significant triumphs and challenging setbacks. A wise man said that we derive the most valuable lessons from our failures rather than our successes. He went on to say that our successes teach us nothing. While I concur with this notion and agree that some of the most profound moments of closeness with God have occurred during periods of intense struggle, opposition, and limited progress, ironically, the birth of this book and the experiences it recounts coincide with a time of unparalleled victory, breakthrough, and accomplishment.

Due to our inherent fallen nature, we are prone to relax and become distracted from God in the wake of success, even though Jesus Christ is the author and finisher of our faith. While our accomplishments may be gratifying, their significance is often fleeting, as Charles Spurgeon aptly described:

> "Emptiness is written on everything until Jesus touches it."
> - Charles Spurgeon

These victories may seem eternal, but without the Lord present to celebrate with us, they will soon fade away like a branch severed from the vine. In this moment, the math no longer adds up—victory resides in the camp, yet an unsettling feeling of emptiness and discontent emerges, transforming into the desert of dissatisfaction. At that moment, I wondered why I felt sad when there was cause for celebration . I realized that God had led me into the desert of dissatisfaction, where I had no accomplishments, victories, or titles. With all distractions silenced, I found complete attunement to Him as He began to speak in a gentle whisper—for I was alone with God.

> "Our work is more than mental work, it is heart work,
> The labour of our inmost soul"
> Charles Spurgeon

We live life on the outside while serving God with our hearts, and so sometimes we can feel like we're losing our way. It's as if, despite our victories, our hearts are under attack, ready to give up, and our defenses are crumbling due to the great void that His absence produces.

The question is, how is it possible to live a life characterized by triumph while simultaneously experiencing profound feelings of unhappiness and discontent?

> "The absence of Christ is hell, but the Presence of Jesus is Heaven."
> - Charles Spurgeon

To prevent this temporary condition from becoming permanent, God gently guides His children into the wilderness of dissatisfaction. Moses, educated in the wisdom of the Egyptians, spent the next forty years in solitude with God, tending a small flock of sheep. He understood that the wilderness was not the end of the world or a sign of God's abandonment, but rather a time when God could connect with him on a deeper level. (Exodus 2:11–15)

> "The dust of victory blinds the eyes that were meant for Jesus."
> - Alex Salcido

> "We pity the poor heathen who adore a god of stone
> And yet we worship victory, a god of gold."
> Charles Spurgeon

Just like with Moses, God draws you and me into the wilderness to remove any obstacles that obscure our communion with Christ. In the wilderness, God stripped Moses of everything Egypt had instilled in him. There, he heard the voice of God, witnessed the burning bush, and discerned the divine call and will for his life. Occasionally, amidst our triumphs, we may be unable to perceive the divine presence or witness His divine glory. To engage with His children, God necessitates their isolation in a wilderness setting. This isolation serves as a means to reveal the path of the Spirit by eliminating distractions, whether positive or negative.

> "Nothing teaches us about the preciousness of the Creator as much as when we learn the emptiness of everything else." - Charles Spurgeon

If you find yourself lost in the desert of dissatisfaction, trust that your Creator has a unique plan in motion for you and is actively shaping your life's journey. Embrace the transformative power of this wilderness! God's love, compassion, and mercy will guide you away from the fleeting joys of success and lead you to true fulfillment.

IN THE END, THE WILDERNESS LEADS US BACK TO A DEEP AND FULFILLING RELATIONSHIP WITH HIS SON, FILLING OUR LIVES WITH ENDLESS JOY AND PEACE.

"When the believer eats the bread of heaven, all the feasts of the Earth seem very flat, stale, and unprofitable."
Charles Spurgeon

"Therefore, behold, I will allure her, and bring her into the wilderness, and speak comfortably unto her. And I will give her her vineyards from thence, and the valley of Achor for a door of hope: and she shall sing there, as in the days of her youth, and as in the day when she came up out of the land of Egypt. And it shall be at that day, saith the LORD, that thou shalt call me Ishi; and shalt call me no more Baali" (Hosea 2:14-16, KJV).

"Faith and hope make the desert like the garden of the Lord."
- Charles Spurgeon

CHAPTER ONE

LURED INTO THE WILDERNESS

"Therefore, behold, I will allure her, and bring her into the wilderness, and speak comfortably unto her. And I will give her her vineyards from thence, and the valley of Achor for a door of hope: and she shall sing there, as in the days of her youth, and as in the day when she came up out of the land of Egypt. And it shall be at that day, saith the LORD, that thou shalt call me Ishi; and shalt call me no more Baali" (Hosea 2:14-16, KJV).

"Into the Wilderness" begins with God redirecting our attention away from His replacement, or what He refers to as "*your many lovers*," and romancing us back to Him. God will use the dissatisfaction of the desert to prepare us for His voice, as the wilderness reveals how meaningless life can be without Him. Unfortunately, we often seek validation from our ministries, titles, and achievements, which only leave us feeling empty and unsatisfied.

> "There cannot be a heaven without a Christ. He is the total of all bliss.
> The fountain from which heaven flows."
> Charles Spurgeon

In the Book of Ecclesiastes, King Solomon explores the concept of vanity, highlighting the futility of seeking happiness without divine involvement. As the wisest, wealthiest, and most influential king in Israel's history, he reflects on life "under the sun" and, from a human perspective, sees it as lacking substance. This realization comes from the deep sense of emptiness that can only be filled by the divine presence of God.

> "Self-confidence only pollutes and dishonors the Savior's work."
> Charles Spurgeon

The Book of Lamentations, often referred to as the funeral of a city, was written during the destruction of Jerusalem, when it was burned to the ground and its inhabitants were taken into Babylonian captivity. It is one of the saddest books of the Bible, where the prophet Jeremiah pleads with God not for the restoration of Jerusalem but for the Lord to turn their hearts back to Him, which would ensure their restoration.

"Turn us back to You, O LORD, and we will be restored; Renew our days as of old" (Lamentations 5:21)

"A jealous God will not be content with a divided heart;

He must be loved first and best. He will withdraw the sunshine of His presence from a cold, wandering heart."
Charles Spurgeon

Restoration and renewal are the result of our journey back to the Lord.

THE ALLURE OF THE WILDERNESS LIES IN THE FACT THAT GOD DOES NOT RESORT TO SHAMING OR JUDGING US BACK TO HIMSELF, BUT RATHER CAPTIVATES OUR HEART WITH HIS MERCY AND STEADFAST LOYAL LOVE.

In the solitude of the wilderness, free from the distractions of worldly noise, we encounter the pure essence of His loyal affection. In these sacred, unadorned spaces, His grace speaks most clearly, inviting us not through fear, condemnation, or shame, but through the tender embrace of His eternal compassion and faithfulness.

"I drew them with gentle cords, with bands of love, and I was to them as those who take the yoke from their neck. I stooped and fed them" (Hosea 11:4).

*"Why do you spend money for what is not bread, and your wages for what does not satisfy? Listen carefully to me, and eat what is good, and let your soul delight itself in abundance. Incline your ear, and come to Me. Hear, and your soul shall live; And **I will make an everlasting covenant with you the sure mercies of David**"* (Isaiah 55:2 & 3).

Pay attention to the fact that God explicitly promises to show us the sure mercies of David. The English word "mercy" used here comes from the Hebrew term "Hesed." Hesed is so profound that no single English word adequately captures its meaning, defying a simple one-word English equivalent. It is impossible to fully comprehend the "sure mercies of David" until one adopts a covenant mindset, which is a result of understanding the full weight of "Hesed."

You find Hesed throughout the Old Testament in different forms. Loyalty, joint obligation, faithfulness, goodness, grace, mercy, lovingkindness, loyal love, favor, godly action, and covenant faithfulness represent the depth and breadth of Hesed.

Kenneth Copeland captured the essence of Hesed when stating: "Lord, You occupy the forefront of my thoughts. My mind and actions are governed by the covenant that binds us together. I yearn to dedicate every moment of my life, from the first day to the last, to fulfilling Your will. Your will has become my will, as we are united in Hesed Covenant." We are children of God in a relationship marked by His eternal lovingkindness, tender mercy, and steadfast loyalty. God is Hesed; His loyalty is unwavering and eternal.

"What is man that You are mindful of him, and the son of man that You visit him" (Psalms 8:4)?

"He who is joined to the Lord is one spirit with Him" (1 Corinthians 6:17).

The Lord assures you that He will never abandon or forsake you. Jesus affirms, "*Even when you exhibit unfaithfulness, I remain steadfast in my faithfulness, for I cannot deny my true nature.*" Since God has entered into a Hesed Covenant with you and me, any achievement or accomplishment that excludes Him leaves us with a sense of dissatisfaction, akin to a hollow victory. Consequently, in His mercy, grace, and love, He draws us into the wilderness, where He can once again become our ultimate source of fulfillment, where He can once again become our "All in all."

*"But then **I will win her back once again**. I will lead her into the desert and speak tenderly to her there"* (Hosea 2:14, NLT).

> "Our love for God is the beautiful offspring of His Love for us."
> - Charles Spurgeon

It is striking to realize that the very feeling of being forsaken can be the pathway through which God's love leads us to rediscover Him.

> *"Behold what manner of love the Father has bestowed on us, that we should be called children of God"* (1 John 3:1)!

> *"There is no fear in love; but perfect love casts out fear, because fear involves torment. But he who fears has not been made perfect in love. We love Him because He first loved us"* (1 John 4:18-19).

> "Spiritual hunger is often dulled by worldly things, and true joy comes from valuing God's glory and presence above all else."
> John Piper

CHAPTER TWO

COMFORT IN THE DESERT

"*Therefore, behold, I will allure her, and bring her into the wilderness, and speak comfortably unto her. And I will give her her vineyards from thence, and the valley of Achor for a door of hope: and she shall sing there, as in the days of her youth, and as in the day when she came up out of the land of Egypt. And it shall be at that day, saith the LORD, that thou shalt call me Ishi; and shalt call me no more Baali*" (Hosea 2:14-16, KJV).

"*I will win her back once again. I will lead her into the desert and speak tenderly to her there*" (Hosea 2:14, NLT)

In the wilderness, God's voice became clear to me as I began to listen more closely. When we finally turn to Him, He fills us with comfort, love, and words of kindness. Remember that our Heavenly Father doesn't scold or shame us back to Himself, but gently draws us with His steadfast, loyal love. With a tender voice, He spoke comfort to me.

"I drew them with gentle cords, With bands of love, And I was to them as those who take the yoke from their neck. I stooped and fed them" (Hosea 11:4).

"Through the Lord's mercies (Hesed) we are not consumed, Because His compassions fail not. [23] They are new every morning; Great is Your faithfulness (Lamentations 3:22-23).

"Turn us back to You, O LORD, and we will be restored; Renew our days as of old (Lamentations 5:21).

Amid my profound sense of dissatisfaction brought about by victory and success, I found solace and comfort when I turned my attention to God. His presence enveloped me, and I felt His loving arms embracing me as a child of God. It was astonishing to witness how His love transcended the wilderness, bringing me back to a place of communion. The familiar voice of compassion resonated with me in the desolate landscape. As I gazed upon Him, His Spirit diverted my attention from my former lovers. I was overwhelmed with awe, and the only words that could emerge from my heart were, "Lord, I have missed You so much. I regret the path I allowed myself to stray on."

*"But then **I will win her back once again**. I will lead her into the desert and speak tenderly to her there"* (Hosea 2:14, NLT).

"A word fitly spoken is like apples of gold in settings of silver" (Proverbs 25:11).

Back in the mid-90s, I took my twelve-year-old son, Alex, on a missionary trip to Suriname. We first flew to British Guyana and then traveled by land to Suriname. Since I was just passing through Guyana, I didn't have any details for a stay there. Upon arrival, a customs agent approached me with routine questions about my purpose of visit and requested my lodging accommodations. Since I had no lodging information, they took us into a room for further interrogation. I explained that I was a minister there to preach and that a pastor friend of mine would pick me up and drive me to Suriname. However, he wasn't convinced of my story and took me into the passenger pickup area while detaining my son to ensure there was "no funny business."

I walked into a large, hot, and humid waiting area, where everyone looked exhausted from the heat and the long wait. Back then, everything was arranged via email, so I didn't even know what the pastor looked like. I was stressed and overwhelmed by the heat and the situation. My thoughts kept drifting to my son and my friend. I also felt intimidated by the large Guyanese customs agent who wouldn't let go of my arm and kept asking where my friend was. I walked in circles, hoping to somehow be recognized by someone I had never met, which only made me look more suspicious. As the agent grew impatient, his tone shifted. But then, from the other side of the hall, I heard a loud shout, "Hello, Alex!" And walking towards us was this Indian Surinamese man with a huge smile.

"Thank you, Jesus! There he is!" I exclaimed. He quickly approached, shook my hand, and started speaking to the customs agent in Dutch. I knew everything was going to be okay. He swiftly calmed things down and explained everything. Everything worked out perfectly, and I was so grateful. You know what? I had never been so happy to hear a familiar voice. I was thrilled to know that, in my helpless situation, God had already provided for my rescue. It was a truly amazing experience that began with a familiar voice.

Likewise, that's what God's soothing voice sounded like to me when I was lost and wandering in my wilderness, going around in circles with this growing dissatisfaction. If you find yourself in the desert of dissatisfaction, it is because God has led you there, in order to reveal His love and call you back to Himself.

SOMETIMES, WHEN WE'RE SERVING THE LORD, WE CAN LOSE SIGHT OF HIM.

In doing the Lord's work, we might lose the Lord. But don't worry, you're doing great and are about to enter a whole new realm in Christ. Newness awaits you as you realize that it's okay to be drawn to Him. He wants to reconnect with you through shared experiences.

"How sweet are Your words to my taste, sweeter than honey to my mouth" (Psalms 119:103)!

"The Spirit Himself bears witness with our spirit that we are children of God, and if children, then heirs—heirs of God and joint heirs with Christ..." (Romans 8:16-17)

We are joint heirs with Christ. Everything that we are, have, and do should be through a full partnership with Him.

"All things were created through Him and for Him. And He is before all things, and in Him all things consist." (Colossians 1:16 & 17).

"Emptiness is written on everything until Jesus touches it."
- Charles Spurgeon

WHEN WE ARE CONNECTED WITH HIM, OUR VICTORIES, SUCCESSES, AND

ACCOMPLISHMENTS BECOME MEANINGFUL.

Remember when Jesus said He came so we could have life and have it more abundantly? He meant that through Him and in Him, we could live life to the fullest, enjoying everything and savoring every moment to the very end. What a glorious thing it is to hear God's gracious voice with the sweet tone of mercy in the arid desert, knowing that everything has been carefully calculated by the Lord to bring you here with good intentions for you.

"For I know the thoughts that I think toward you, says the LORD, thoughts of peace and not of evil, to give you a future and a hope. 12 Then you will call upon Me and go and pray to Me, and I will listen to you. 13 And you will seek Me and find Me, when you search for Me with all your heart." (Jeremiah 29:11-13).

"HOPE is like a star. It is not seen in the sunshine of prosperity, and only to be discovered in the night of adversity."
Charles Spurgeon

CHAPTER THREE

VINEYARDS IN THE WILDERNESS

*"Therefore, behold, I will allure her, and bring her into the wilderness, and speak comfortably unto her. And **I will give her her vineyards from thence,** and the valley of Achor for a door of hope: and she shall sing there, as in the days of her youth, and as in the day when she came up out of the land of Egypt. And it shall be at that day, saith the LORD, that thou shalt call me Ishi; and shalt call me no more Baali"* (Hosea 2:14-16, KJV).

Once He speaks comfort, the Lord gives us vineyards right in the midst of the desert. Just remember, these vineyards are ours. These are promises that God has made to us and is ready to fulfill without a moment's hesitation.

Vineyards produce wine, and the new wine that the Bible talks about represents the New Testament blessings. It signifies a transformation of heart and spirit, and the outpouring of the Holy Ghost. It represents the transformative power of Christ that cannot be confined by the old, rigid structures of the law. It also signifies the grace of God, oneness with the Holy Spirit, and joining the Royal Household of God (Matthew 9:14-17, Mark 2:18-22, and Luke 5:33-39). All these benefits, and more, are the product of the vineyards gifted to us in the desert of dissatisfaction.

In this place, God promises a fresh outpouring of the Holy Spirit in our lives, where our oneness with Him becomes an undeniable reality. He guides us on a journey, elevating us from one level of glory to an even greater one. With each step, He reveals the boundless depths of His grace, a transformative grace so profound that it transcends our present condition, opening our hearts and minds to a greater glory. Now we begin to see how

---

BEING LURED INTO THE WILDERNESS WAS GOD'S WAY OF RELEASING THE NEW WINE BACK INTO OUR LIVES.

> "The deeper a man drinks into the spirit of Christ,
> the happier he will become."
> Charles Spurgeon

"not by works of righteousness which we have done, but according to His mercy He saved us" (Titus 3:5),

The New Testament blessings reveal that we can live free from guilt, condemnation, emptiness, and dissatisfaction. By placing our complete trust in the finished work of Christ, our Savior, we can fully enjoy life, knowing that by God's grace, we are who we are, do what we do, and achieve what we achieve.

We understand that we have an eternal promise with our Father, fully paid for by the blood of His Son. We are heirs with God and joint heirs with Christ, in a full partnership in everything related to life and godliness.

Oh, and He promised us vineyards! Not just one vineyard, but vineyards! Can you imagine? Enough vineyards to make new wine forever. We are living in the age of the dispensation of Grace that will take us from glory to glory in this life and the next. You see, these vineyards are eternal, for they're not like the fleeting joys of life's victories without God. Praise the Lord! Let's open our minds and hearts to this new way of thinking and living. Embrace the transformative power of Jesus' new wine, and let go of the old victories that don't truly satisfy.

"Brethren, we do not want merely to go to heaven, but we desire to enjoy our heaven on the road to heaven"
Charles Spurgeon

CHAPTER FOUR

A DOOR OF HOPE

"Therefore, behold, I will allure her, and bring her into the wilderness, and speak comfortably unto her. And I will give her her vineyards from thence, **and the valley of Achor for a door of hope:** *and she shall sing there, as in the days of her youth, and as in the day when she came up out of the land of Egypt. And it shall be at that day, saith the LORD, that thou shalt call me Ishi; and shalt call me no more Baali"* (Hosea 2:14-16, KJV).

Once we catch a glimpse of the vineyards that produce the New Wine of the Gospel of grace, God continues to speak life, hope, and breakthrough into our desert.

When God mentioned the Valley of Achor to the Israelites, they knew exactly what He was referring to. Recall the book of Joshua during the conquest of the Promised Land. The first city they conquered was Jericho. They had specific instructions: nothing was to be taken, and everything was to be burned down. Jericho was the first fruit of all the conquered lands.

"But the children of Israel committed a trespass regarding the accursed things, for Achan the son of Carmi, the son of Zabdi, the son of Zerah, of the tribe of Judah, took of the accursed things; so the anger of the LORD burned against the children of Israel… v20 And Achan answered Joshua and said, "Indeed I have sinned against the LORD God of Israel, and this is what I have done" (Joshua 7:1 & 20)

Achan's secret transgression led to a national defeat for Israel when they faced the significantly smaller and inferior army of Ai. In their state of defeat, they sought God's guidance to understand the cause of this dire situation. Through a process of elimination, Achan and his transgression were revealed. The Valley of Achor became the site where Achan and his family were stoned to death for taking the "accursed things." The children of Israel associated this valley with defeat, anguish, confusion, curses, sadness, feelings of abandonment, and the loss of loved ones.

Besides drawing you into the desert where God spoke comfort and provided vineyards, He also promises to transform the Valley of Achor into a door of hope. Any defeat, failure, or struggle in your life can be likened to the Valley of Achor, but God has promised to turn it into a door of hope.

" Hope is like a star. It is not seen in the sunshine of prosperity,
and only to be discovered in the night of adversity."
Charles Spurgeon

Wow!

ONLY GOD CAN TRANSFORM THE DESERT OF DISSATISFACTION AND DEFEAT INTO A DOOR OF HOPE.

You are finally seeing the light at the end of the tunnel. If God is for you, who can be against you? This lack of joy, unhappiness, and dissatisfaction was His way of drawing you into the desert so He could comfort you, give you vineyards, and turn your Valley of Achor into a door of hope.

God is so sovereign over the disasters and disappointments of our lives that He is able to take all of them and make all of them serve our everlasting joy. This sovereign grace is the ground of joy in the sorrows of deep disappointment. We seek joy in our sorrows so that the essence of our life becomes a bittersweet symphony of sorrow and joy - John Piper

"And we know that all things work together for good to those who love God, to those who are the called according to His purpose" (Romans 8:28).

"...with God all things are possible" (Matthew 19:26).

Here are a few of my favorite Bible verses that I find especially meaningful when ministering to individuals facing challenging circumstances:

"Come, and let us return to the LORD; for He has torn, but He will heal us; He has stricken, but He will bind us up. After two days He will revive us; On the third day He will raise us up, that we may live in His sight. Let us know, let us pursue the knowledge of the LORD. His going forth is established as the morning; He will come to us like the rain, Like the latter and former rain to the earth" (Hosea 6:1-3).

"Cause me to hear Your lovingkindness in the morning, For in You do I trust" (Psalms 143:8);

"Revive me, O Lord, for Your name's sake! For Your righteousness' sake bring my soul out of trouble" (Psalms 143:11).

"Heal me, O LORD, and I shall be healed; Save me, and I shall be saved, For You are my praise" (Jeremiah 17:14).

"Lord deliver us from any sort of reliance upon ourselves, whatever shape the reliance might take."
 - Charles Spurgeon

CHAPTER FIVE

SINGING ONCE AGAIN

"Therefore, behold, I will allure her, and bring her into the wilderness, and speak comfortably unto her. And I will give her her vineyards from thence, and the valley of Achor for a door of hope: and **she shall sing there, as in the days of her youth, and as in the day when she came up out of the land of Egypt.** *And it shall be at that day, saith the LORD, that thou shalt call me Ishi; and shalt call me no more Baali"* (Hosea 2:14-16, KJV).

When the Lord restores us to the blessings of His new wine, everything begins to make sense. As we step through the door of Hope, joy returns to our lives, and we begin singing once again.

There are two things about the song that He places in our hearts. He promises that we will sing like when we were young and full of life.

A NEW SONG ERUPTS FROM THE DEPTHS OF OUR SOULS, AND WE BEGIN SINGING JUST LIKE WHEN WE WERE FIRST CONVERTED.

Remember how joyful our hearts were when we were first saved? Everything was new, vibrant, and beautiful. There's nothing quite like the feeling of a fresh start. The old had passed away, and all things had become new. We couldn't be silenced or stopped from sharing our faith because God had done incredible things in us, and they were so real and new. That's where God is taking us on this journey. He's not just the source of joy; He is all joy.

> "Our Happy God should be worshipped by happy people."
> Charles Spurgeon

Singing once again involves fresh infillings with the Holy Spirit. It's fascinating how being filled with the Spirit leads to singing and making melody in our hearts. Spontaneous gratitude creates a beautiful melody within us. And guess what? He's promising to bring that back into our lives!

> "When Jesus comes into the heart, He issues a general license to be glad in the Lord.

No chains are worn in the court of King Jesus."
Charles Spurgeon

"And do not be drunk with wine, in which is dissipation; but be filled with the Spirit, speaking to one another in psalms and hymns and spiritual songs, singing and making melody in your heart to the Lord, giving thanks always for all things to God the Father in the name of our Lord Jesus Christ, submitting to one another in the fear of God" (Ephesians 5:18-21).

You would sing as you did when freed from the bondage and slavery of Egypt. Jesus paid too high a price to leave you stranded in enemy territory. The Father loves you too much to leave you searching for answers in an unending desert.

The one hundred twenty-sixth psalm beautifully depicts the overwhelming joy of God's people upon their return from Babylonian exile. Imagine the sheer exhilaration of receiving permission to go home, rebuild the temple, and worship God as they had longed to. The Persian king Cyrus went above and beyond, providing everything needed for the project. It must have felt surreal, almost unbelievable, to them, and their hearts likely burst with joy.

"When the LORD brought back the captivity of Zion, **we were like those who dream.** *Then our mouth was filled with laughter, and our tongue with singing. Then they said among the nations, "The LORD has*

done great things for them." The LORD has done great things for us, and we are glad' (Psalms 126:1-3).

That's the immense grace and abundant provision God offers to those who return to Him. I know that feeling all too well, as I experienced it firsthand when God gave me a general license to rejoice. We've gained from our struggles in the past, and we will gain from our victories as well. The happiness derived from accomplishments is magnified when it brings people closer to God. His presence alone is the source of boundless joy and true satisfaction.

"You will show me the path of life; In Your presence is fullness of joy; At Your right hand are pleasures forevermore" (Psalms 16:11).

Have you ever wondered if it's possible to return to that place in the Lord where you could sing and rejoice like you did when you were first saved? A place where sharing your faith with others was a spontaneous act? Well, let me tell you, God is with you and for you, and He has the power to restore you and give you more than you could ever think or imagine. He is a God of glory, and He is taking you on a journey from glory to glory.

God, "is able to do exceedingly abundantly above all that we ask or think, according to the power that works in us" (Ephesians 3:20),

"But we all, with unveiled face, beholding as in a mirror the glory of the Lord, are being transformed

into the same image from glory to glory, just as by the Spirit of the Lord" (2 Corinthians 3:18).

"So all of us who have had that veil removed can see and reflect the glory of the Lord. And the Lord—who is the Spirit—makes us more and more like him as we are changed into his glorious image" (2 Corinthians 3:18, NLT)

> "We are leaky vessels, and we must keep right under the fountain all the time to be kept full."
> D.L. Moody

CHAPTER SIX

From Master to Husband

"*Therefore, behold, I will allure her, and bring her into the wilderness, and speak comfortably unto her. And I will give her her vineyards from thence, and the valley of Achor for a door of hope: and she shall sing there, as in the days of her youth, and as in the day when she came up out of the land of Egypt. And it shall be at that day, saith the LORD, that thou shalt call me Ishi; and shalt call me no more Baali*" (Hosea 2:14-16, KJV).

Right here, our relationship with God undergoes a profound transformation, taking on a new form. Our perception of God shifts from a distant master to that of a loving and caring husband.

In some Middle Eastern countries, marriages are traditionally arranged by parents. Often, the bride and groom haven't met in person and have only exchanged pictures. As they embark on their journey together, feelings for each other gradually develop over time. The wife affectionately addresses her husband as "Baali," meaning "my master." As they live side by side, they nurture a genuine love for one another through shared experiences, triumphs, and challenges. Over time, the wife's affectionate tone evolves, and she begins to call him "Ishi," meaning "my husband." This transformative change redefines the relationship, infusing it with a deeper sense of purpose and meaning.

"And it shall be, in that day," Says the Lord, "That you will call Me 'My Husband,' And no longer call Me 'My Master (Hosea 2:16),

I recall a time when I faced challenges in my marriage. The things that once worked were no longer effective, and my wife and I were at a breaking point. I sought God's wisdom and guidance, hoping to improve our situation, but nothing seemed to work. Despite my best efforts and deep love for my wife, nothing resonated. I felt lost and hopeless, with no answers in sight.

One morning, I was awakened by the Spirit and compelled to pray. In desperation, I rushed to the living room and began praying in tongues, English, and Spanish until I felt His presence descending upon me. It was as if God was healing a wound in my heart and restoring my mind. He revealed that my marriage problems stemmed from my relationship with Him.

Surprisingly, instead of shaming or condemning me, God spoke to me with mercy, grace, and love. He guided me to a place of comfort and healing, transforming the Valley of Achor into a door of hope. God liberated me from bondage and reminded me of His unwavering love. A profound transformation occurred that morning. A new kind of love emerged from the depths of my soul—a love that transcended the familiar "Baali" (my master) to the profound "Ishi" (my husband). My bond with God deepened immeasurably, and my intimacy with the Almighty grew exponentially. Something supernatural occurred, so profound that it forever changed my relationship with Him.

I felt like the children of Israel when God called them out of Babylon, as if I were in a dream, filled with laughter and joy.

I EXPERIENCED A SIDE OF GOD'S LOVE THAT I HAD NEVER KNOWN BEFORE, AND FROM THAT MOMENT ON, MY MARRIAGE BEGAN TO HEAL AND BLOSSOM.

I started singing out loud, just like I did during my new convert days. I was transported back to that place of newfound faith, as if I were in a dream, filled with laughter and joy, all thanks to the extraordinary love I had come to experience.

God can indeed help your marriage, family, and relationships. Everything in the desert of dissatisfaction has led to this revelation of God's manifold love.

> "God's love manifests itself in a multifaceted manner, compared to a diamond with boundless sides and angles. As one believes they have gained familiarity with His love, the diamond turns and transforms, revealing an entirely novel side of God's Love."
> Joy Dawson

"When the LORD brought back the captivity of Zion, we were like those who dream. Then our mouth was filled with laughter, and our tongue with singing. Then they said among the nations, "The LORD has done great things for them." The LORD has done great things for us, and we are glad" (Psalms 126:1-3).

It is a profoundly meaningful revelation to glimpse into a hidden dimension of God. It's like discovering a hidden treasure trove of love! The unwavering, steadfast loyalty of this love brings immense comfort, joy, and solace.

Just like King David, when he sought to find if there were any descendants of Jonathan, King Saul's son, so that he could show them Kindness (Covenant Faithfulness), so Jesus, our King, continues to seek us out in the desert of dissatisfaction to show us covenant faithfulness.

Christ wants to show you Hesed. He has nothing but good intentions in mind when it comes to you, your family, and your ministry. He is looking to elevate your love and service towards Him to another level. (2 Samuel 9:1)

"Sing, O barren, You who have not borne! Break forth into singing, and cry aloud, You who have not labored with child! For more are the children of the desolate than the children of the married woman," says the LORD. "Enlarge the place of your tent, And let them stretch out the curtains of your dwellings; Do not spare; Lengthen your cords, And strengthen your stakes. For you shall expand to the right and to the left, And your descendants will inherit the nations, And make the desolate cities inhabited" (Isaiah 54:1-3).

> "Barrenness is the platform for His fruit-creating power. "
> Charles Spurgeon

"For I know the thoughts that I think toward you, says the LORD, thoughts of peace and not of evil, to give you a future and a hope" (Jeremiah 29:11).

> I will go in helplessness,
>
> I will go in all my shame and backsliding,
>
> I will tell Him that I am still His child,
>
> And in confidence in His faithful heart,
>
> I, even I, the barren one, will sing and cry aloud once again.

You've been drawn into the wilderness, so listen closely to His soothing voice, which seeks to comfort you. He has given you vineyards, transforming all defeat and dissatisfaction into a doorway of hope. It is here where you will sing as you did in your early days of faith, changing a master–servant relationship into a loving husband-and-wife relationship.

CHAPTER SEVEN

THE HUSBAND'S CALL

"Therefore, behold, I will allure her, and bring her into the wilderness, and speak comfortably unto her. And I will give her her vineyards from thence, and the valley of Achor for a door of hope: and she shall sing there, as in the days of her youth, and as in the day when she came up out of the land of Egypt. ***And it shall be at that day, saith the LORD, that thou shalt call me Ishi; and shalt call me no more Baali"*** (Hosea 2:14-16, KJV).

"Behold, I stand at the door and knock. If anyone hears My voice and opens the door, I will come in to him and dine with him, and he with Me" (Revelation 3:20).

Dear Reader,

The stage is set, and the feast is prepared. God is ready to pour out His Spirit upon you, renewing you and infusing your triumphs with life.

> "There cannot be a heaven without a Christ. He is the sum total of all bliss,
>
> The fountain from which heaven flows."
> Charles Spurgeon

Come to Me, all you who labor and are heavy laden, and I will give you rest. ^{29} Take My yoke upon you and learn from Me, for I am gentle and lowly in heart, and you will find rest for your souls. ^{30} For My yoke is easy and My burden is light" (Matthew 11:28-30).

Jesus Christ is not merely looking to restore you to your former glory; He desires for you to experience a whole new facet of His love. The reason He drew you to read this book, and why it resonated with you, is to elevate your understanding of Him, taking you from a place of reverence to one of intimacy and companionship. Jesus can turn even the darkest valleys into places of hope and joy. He is knocking at your heart, calling you to come to Him. He has a plan for you, a path to an abundant life.

"Until the Spirit is poured upon us from on high, And the wilderness becomes a fruitful field, And the fruitful field is counted as a forest" (Isaiah 32:15).

"Every person has a duty to worship and love God, and we cannot fulfill this important responsibility properly unless our hearts are filled with love for God and our connection with Him is so strong that it compels us to turn to Him constantly, just like young children who cannot stand without their mother's loving embrace."

- Beaufort (modern English)

Your Husband is inviting you to partake of His divine Presence once more. Allow Him to infuse you with the profound experience I am referring to. An extraordinary transformation awaits! Confidently pray this prayer, believing that He will elevate you to unimaginable heights . The Holy Spirit will unveil Jesus and God's love in a manner that surpasses all your previous experiences.

GOD HAS PATIENTLY AWAITED THIS MOMENT TO TRANSFORM YOUR SERVANT--MASTER DYNAMIC INTO A PROFOUND AND LOVING HUSBAND-WIFE RELATIONSHIP.

Here is the Prayer:

Dear Wonderful Jesus, I am so grateful for the Hesed covenant that You brought me into. I am humbled that You would take the time and effort to lure me into the wilderness just to meet with me.

Fill me once again with Your Presence and unveil another dimension of Your love that I have yet to experience. I eagerly accept Your invitation and, with open arms, I embark on this journey with You.

I entrust You with transforming our relationship from a servant–master dynamic to a husband–wife bond. I offer You my unwavering devotion and receive Yours by faith. Lead me in the way of everlasting, and I shall follow You anywhere. I receive all that You have bestowed upon me and will keep You at the forefront of my thoughts. In Jesus' mighty name, amen.

Hallelujah, thank You Jesus, praise the Lord! Congratulations!

Like the lyrics of the old hymn, "He Touched Me" say,

> "He touched me, Oh, He touched me
>
> And oh, the joy that floods my soul
>
> Something happened, and now I know
>
> He touched me and made me whole."

You better believe that something happened. While it defies rational explanation, it can only be experienced firsthand.

> "The Power reveals what God can do.

The Presence reveals who God is."
Claudion Friedzon

You have experienced the power in times past, but today you experienced the Presence. Congratulations! Be filled with excitement and eagerly anticipate the incredible journey that lies ahead. May you be blessed with all the love and favor bestowed upon you.

"Sing, O barren, You who have not borne! Break forth into singing, and cry aloud, You who have not labored with child! For more are the children of the desolate than the children of the married woman," says the Lord. 2 "Enlarge the place of your tent, And let them stretch out the curtains of your dwellings; Do not spare; Lengthen your cords, And strengthen your stakes" (Isaiah 54:1-2).

"No longer do I call you servants, for a servant does not know what his master is doing; but I have called you friends, for all things that I heard from My Father I have made known to you. 16 You did not choose Me, but I chose you and appointed you that you should go and bear fruit, and that your fruit should remain, that whatever you ask the Father in My name He may give you" (John 15:15 & 16).

CHAPTER EIGHT

DISCIPLINES THAT MAKE MY LIFE

"Spiritual practices worth keeping produce a constant awareness of God." — A. Salcido

"In all your ways acknowledge Him, And He shall direct your paths" (Proverbs 3:6).

"Listen for God's voice in everything you do, everywhere you go; he's the one who will keep you on track" (Proverbs 3:6, The Message Bible).

"The time of business does not differ with me from the time of prayer, and in the noise and clatter of my kitchen, while several persons are at the same time calling for different things, I possess God in as great tranquility as if I were on my knees at the blessed sacrament."
Brother Lawrence

"Spiritual practices worth keeping produce a constant awareness of God." — A. Salcido

- My Morning Arrows are scriptures that jump out at me when reading His Word.

In my reading of God's Word, whenever a verse jumps out at me, I immediately highlight it and text it to myself for later reflection or use in prayer. You see, I know that those verses of scripture are going to assist me in prayer that morning. As I pray and these "morning arrows" come to mind, I immediately bring out my phone and start reading and incorporating those scriptures into my prayers.

"So shall My word be that goes forth from My mouth; It shall not return to Me void, But it shall accomplish what I please, And it shall prosper in the thing for which I sent it" (Isaiah 55:11).

"Your word is a lamp to my feet And a light to my path" (Psalm 119:105).

They're useful for the day's challenges and ministry.

Assuredly, I say to you, till heaven and earth pass away, one jot or one tittle will by no means pass from the law till all is fulfilled (Matthew 5:18).

God knows what life will bring that day or whom He will bring in my direction for ministry, so His living word customizes itself for the occasion.

> "We must shoot the Lord's arrows right back at him."
> Charles Spurgeon

I always try to take time and reflect on my morning arrows, and as I go through them, not only is my soul nourished, but people come to mind that I am to share them with.

- Quick Moments of Supplication throughout the Day.

These are times throughout the day when I stop what I'm doing and bring prayers and supplications before the Lord.

For example, suppose that morning was a time when I felt the need to pray for specific things. In that case, I partner with the Holy Spirit in short bursts of prayer and supplication throughout the day.

"Ask, and it will be given to you; seek, and you will find; knock, and it will be opened to you. For everyone who asks receives, and he who seeks finds, and to him who knocks it will be opened" (Matthew 7:7 & 8).

> "Every believer should embrace the practice of spontaneous prayer."
> Charles Spurgeon

- Quick Moments of Communion.

"The grace of the Lord Jesus Christ, and the love of God, and the communion of the Holy Spirit be with you all. Amen" (2 Corinthians 13:14).

Communion in Greek is Koinonia, which has seven different meanings.

Presence

Fellowship—getting to know each other as friends.

Sharing together.

Participate together.

Intimacy—The oneness and union with the Holy Spirit.

Friendship.

Comradeship—one who is fighting with you in battle.

–Benny Hinn

"Every person has a duty to worship and love God, and we cannot fulfill this important responsibility properly unless our hearts are filled with love for God and our connection with Him is so strong that it compels us to turn to Him constantly, just like young children who cannot stand without their mother's loving embrace."

- Beaufort (modern English)

As I go about the day, I purposely make time for quick moments of communion with the Holy Spirit. In whatever I do, I pause, close my eyes, and acknowledge His presence with terms of endearment such as: *"I love You, Lord. Thank you, Jesus, that You love me. Holy Spirit, commune with me. I acknowledge You in my life. Father, Your son worships You."*

"We should cease for one brief moment as often as we can

To worship God in the depth of our being.

To taste him though it be in passing.

To touch him as it were by stealth."

— Brother Lawrence

A company I worked for would encourage its workers to take "Micro-brakes." This meant taking a few minutes to straighten up or to get out of the elements to clear your mind before returning to the task. These two to three-minute (micro breaks) would do wonders for the individual mentally and physically. Likewise, we must learn to take micro-breaks throughout our day and be aware of His Presence.

"Faith is our walk, but fellowship is our rest.
Faith is the road, but communion with Jesus is the well from which the pilgrim drinks."
Charles Spurgeon

God, the Holy Spirit, wants to spend intimate moments with you throughout the day. It's more than just a ritual or things Christians do; it's what we are.

You will show me the path of life; In Your presence is fullness of joy; At Your right hand are pleasures forevermore (Psalm 16:11).

For a day in Your courts is better than a thousand. I would rather be a doorkeeper in the house of my God than dwell in the tents of wickedness. (Psalm 84:10).

"You can't go forward in life without drenching every step in prayer.

Pray without ceasing."
Charles Spurgeon

- My cup runs over.

You anoint my head with oil; My cup runs over (Psalm 23:5).

These mornings and awareness of His presence throughout the day produce anticipation in the service of His people. There's this eagerness to pour myself out and be a messenger of hope, grace, encouragement, and blessing to those the Lord brings in my direction.

Heal the sick, cleanse the lepers, raise the dead, cast out demons. Freely you have received, freely give (Matthew 10:8).

I will very gladly spend and be spent for your souls (2 Corinthians 12:15).

You are the light of the world (Matthew 5:14).

Wherever I go and whatever I do, I always look for opportunities to impart grace to the hearer, to inject courage into a discouraged believer, to speak life and hope into the unconverted, and to lead those who hunger and thirst to a land flowing with milk and honey.

Let your speech always be with grace, seasoned with salt, that you may know how you ought to answer each one (Colossians 4:6).

The LORD God has given me the tongue of the learned, that I should know how to speak a word in season to him who is weary (Isaiah 50:4).

"Imitate divine wisdom, and encourage others." – Charles Spurgeon

- I make it a point to live in the reality that God is in everything, and He can speak to me at any moment.

"Position yourself to hear from God

And He can speak to you through anything." – Bill Johnson

Hearing from God is every believer's God-given right. He can speak to you through anything or anyone.

My sheep hear My voice, and I know them, and they follow Me (John 10:27).

"It is the nature of God to speak." – A. W. Tozer

I POSITION MYSELF TO HEAR FROM GOD BY SIMPLY BELIEVING THAT IF I PAY CLOSE ATTENTION TO LIFE, HE WILL SPEAK TO ME WHEREVER I AM.

At any given moment, the Lord can speak through people, circumstances, and places.

I remember, as a young pastor going through a rough season, my home was being assaulted. I was not seeing the results I wanted to see. My finances were in shambles, and my mind was plagued with head trip after head trip. I was standing on my front lawn, leaning on the fence, watching my son Julius, who at the time was around six, playing in the yard barefoot. I was in deep thought, reflecting and talking to the Lord, when suddenly he came up to me and asked the most bizarre question.

He said. "*Dad, God doesn't always answer prayer, does he?*"

I was surprised by such a question, especially from a six-year-old. After a long pause, I reluctantly said, "*Sure, he does.*"

He replied, "*No, He doesn't, because sometimes I get little cuts on my toes, and I ask Him to heal them and they don't go away.*"

Instinctively, I said, "*Yes, He does, son. Don't the cuts eventually go away just like you asked? You see, Julius, God always comes through, even if it takes a while.*"

He looked at me full of faith, and pleased with the answer, he walked away happy.

Wow, at that instant, I heard from God, and I knew exactly what He meant. The great God of Abraham, Isaac, and Jacob met with me through my son and then used my voice to reaffirm His faithfulness.

An infinite God can give all of Himself to each of His children.

He does not distribute Himself that each may have a part, but to each one He gives all of Himself as fully as if there were no others. — A.W. Tozer

"God is in everything."

He is before all things, and in Him all things consist (Colossians 1:17).

As a musician, I enjoy listening to music. I don't just hear it; I listen. I love to hear the chord progressions, the beat, and the different instruments playing. I pay attention to whole notes, half notes, quarter notes, eighth notes, and so on. Is the song in a minor or major key? How are the vocals and harmonies? In other words, if I merely hear the song, I miss most of its beauty, but if I listen, I can fully appreciate the composition. Likewise, we must make it our aim to listen for God's voice in life, lest we miss creation speaking on His behalf.

Brother Lawrence, born in French Lorraine in the 17th century, made it his life's calling to serve in the kitchen, preparing meals and cleaning up. Before beginning his duties, he was known for praying this prayer:

"Lord of all pots and pans and things,

make me a saint by getting meals and washing up the plates!" - Brother Lawrence

"Thus, Brother Lawrence was able to turn even the most commonplace and menial task into a living hymn to the glory of God." Let us take a page from Brother Lawrence's book, who was so conscious of God in everything that he would find Him even in the most ordinary tasks.

For since the creation of the world, God's invisible qualities, his eternal power and divine nature have been clearly seen, being understood from what has been made (Romans 1:20 NIV)

ENDNOTES: Brother Lawrence in "*Practice of the Presence of God.*" (Grand Rapids, MI: Spire Books, 1998.)

CHAPTER NINE

AUTHOR'S BIOGRAPHY

Pastor/Author Alex Salcido and his wife, Lorena, are the senior pastors of New Destiny Christian Church in Northridge, California, USA. They lead a growing community of believers passionate about revival, healing for the body of Christ, world missions, and the lost coming to salvation. Their ministry is carried out through Home, Satellite, and Online Churches. They have been blessed with four children and currently have six grandchildren.

In 1978, Alex had a miraculous experience when he first heard the Gospel of Jesus Christ at the park. After several years of searching, he was eventually led to New Destiny Christian Church in El Centro, California, in 1982, and the rest is history.

Alex, having emerged from a past shrouded in sin and bondage, was miraculously delivered, healed, and restored from every imaginable form of enslavement. At the tender age of 15, he received the divine call to preach the Gospel of Jesus Christ. In 1992, he embarked on a journey to pioneer a church in the San Fernando Valley, a mission that continues to this day. During his "Tour of Duty," Alex has successfully established six new churches within the United States and three international works.

His Kingdom ventures have taken him throughout the United States, Mexico, Colombia, Venezuela, Suriname, British Guyana, Peru, Ecuador, and Europe. His ministry is characterized by the supernatural power of God, which is reflected in the countless individuals who have come to Christ, as well as in the miracles, signs, and wonders. His passion is evident in every setting, whether preaching to a small group of believers in the jungle or large crowds at his Healing and Deliverance Crusades.

Alex and his wife, Lorena, lead a ministry dedicated to liberating captives and infusing their listeners with joy, hope, and power. As Alex puts it, "With God's Word, we can reach into the depths of a person's soul and remove anything that may hinder spiritual, mental, emotional, or physical health." God's Word is alive and has the power to transform lives from the uttermost to the uttermost.

He is well-known for delivering messages that offer hope, healing, restoration, and deliverance. He delights in preaching about the Father, the Son, and the Holy Ghost, emphasizing that the supernatural should be a regular occurrence in the lives of believers and the Church of Jesus Christ.

His motto is,

> # "NO ONE IS EVER TOO FAR GONE FOR JESUS. THERE IS ALWAYS HOPE!"

The Spirit of the Lord is upon Me, Because He has anointed Me To preach the gospel to the poor; *He has sent Me* to heal the brokenhearted, *To proclaim liberty to the captives And recovery of sight to the blind, To set at liberty those who are* oppressed; *To proclaim the acceptable year of the Lord* (Luke 4:18-19).

As he continues his pastoral calling, Alex actively engages in several social media ministries to encourage the body of Christ to live in victory and reach out to the lost. He remains steadfast in his commitment to remind God's people of His unwavering love, grace, and willingness to save them completely.

Several years ago, he launched a worldwide Mentoring/Apprenticeship course for new preachers and aspiring ministers. The objective is to train and equip the next generation of preachers.

Here are some of his favorite sayings.

There is always Hope!

You're doing good.

Your prayers have Power.

Nothing is impossible for my God.

Let's pray.

God is about to touch you!

It's On!

Be filled!

He will fix you.

CHAPTER TEN

ADDITIONAL RESOURCES
Available
In english and Spanish

Additional invaluable Resources

In addition are invaluable resources provided by Pastor Alex's sister, Lupita Salcido Vizcarra. Her profound supernatural ministry and prophetic voice stand as a beacon for our generation. Lupita's ministry is deeply rooted in spiritual discernment, marked by transformative encounters and divine revelations that prepare hearts for the coming revival. Her prophetic insight not only speaks to individual lives but also resounds across communities, igniting faith and inspiring a deeper pursuit of God's presence.

Through her teachings, Lupita empowers believers to recognize and respond to the movements of the Holy Spirit, fostering an environment where miracles, healings, and prophetic words are not just expected but experienced. Her dedication to nurturing spiritual growth and awakening a hunger for righteousness makes her contribution to this generation both timely and transformative.Lupe Salcido-Vizcarra, PL-Faith, A Servant of Jesus Christ, called and sent by God as a Prophetic Voice for our Generation, to bring His Message to The Church and to the world as God wills.

Preaching, Teaching, Healing, Saving, Establishing the Kingdom of God on earth. She is the Founder of Kingdom Ministries, a Global Evangelistic organization reaching the world with Hope, Salvation, Love & Power of CHRIST, Connecting the world to JESUS. Ministries include Miracle Crusades, HopeWithJesus.com, Radio & TV, online School, Channels, Women Ministries. She is Co-Pastor with Her Husband, Pastor Renato Vizcarra, at Power of The Gospel Church.

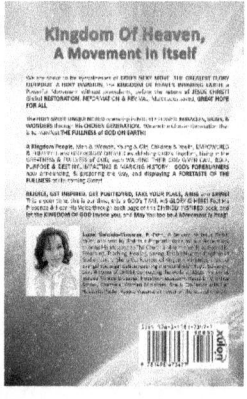
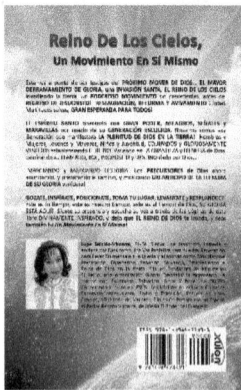

Author YouTube:

https://youtube.com/@authoralexandersalcido

https://youtube.com/@newdestinychurchofthevalley

Author Facebook

Facebook.comauthoralexandersalcido

Facebook NEW DESTINY

facebook.com/ndvannuys

Author Instagram

Instragram.com/.authoralexandersalcido

Instagram NEW DESTINY

instagram.com/newdestinychurchpc

Author TikTok

TikTok.com/.authoralexandersalcido

https://www.tiktok.com/@newdestinyvalleychurch

https://alexandersalcido.com/

https://newdestinychurchpc.com/

www.ingramcontent.com/pod-product-compliance
Lightning Source LLC
Chambersburg PA
CBHW060426050426
42449CB00009B/2153